MY COOL ROOM

THINGS TO MAKE AND DO!

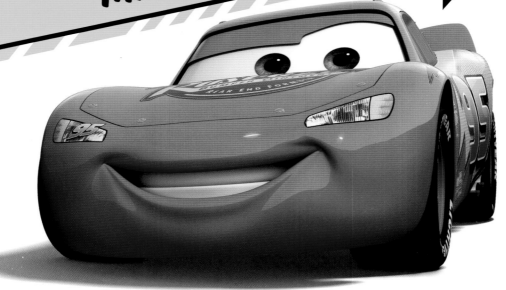

PaRragon

Bath • New York • Singapore • Hong Kong • Cologne • Delhi
Melbourne • Amsterdam • Johannesburg • Auckland • Shenzhen

First edition published by Parragon in 2011

Parragon
Queen Street House
4 Queen Street
Bath BA1 1HE, UK

ISBN 978-1-4454-1804-9

Printed in China

CONTENTS

TIPS FOR SUCCESS

Remember, everything in this book should be mad with the supervision and help of a grown up! A ste labeled with "Kids" means that a child can do thi step on their own. Some items will need to be purchase from a supermarket or a craft/hobby store.

1 Prepare your space

Cover your work space with newspaper or a plastic or paper tablecloth. Make sure you and your children are wearing clothes (including shoes!) that you don't mind getting splattered with food, paint, or glue. But relax! You'll never completely avoid mess; in fact, it's part of the fun!

2 Wash your hands

Wash your hands before starting a new project, and clean up as you go along. Clean hands make for clean crafts! Remember to wash hands afterwards too, using soap and warm water to remove any of the remaining materials.

3 Follow steps carefully

Follow each step carefully, and in the sequence in which it appears. We've tested all the projects; we know they work, and we want them to work for you, too.

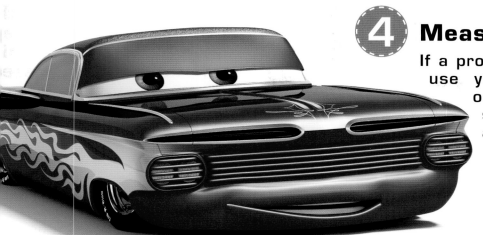

4 Measure precisely

If a project gives you measurements, use your ruler, measuring cups, or measuring spoons to make sure you measure as accurately as you can. Sometimes, the success of the project may depend on it.

5 Be patient

You may need to wait while allowing paint, glue, or clay to dry, sometimes for a few hours or even overnight. Be patient! Plan another activity while you wait, but it's important not to rush something as it may affect the outcome!

6 Clean up

When you've finished your project, clean up any mess. Store all the materials together so that they are ready for the next time you want to make a craft. Remember it's a team effort!

TIRE TRACK FRAME

Mack has the biggest tires since he is one big truck! Create this tire themed frame to show off your favorite pictures!

YOU WILL NEED

- THICK CARD (CARDBOARD BOX)
- MASKING TAPE
- TOY CAR OR TRUCK
- PAINTS
- SMALL SPONGE
- SAFETY SCISSORS

1

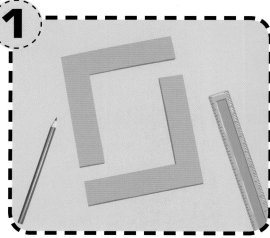

Cut 2 'L' shapes from card that is about 8 x 1½ inches in size.

2

Tape the two pieces together to make a frame then paint it black. Allow to dry.

Kids 3

Sponge paint onto the wheels of a toy car or truck then roll it around the frame slowly pressing down so it leaves a clear track mark.

Wipe the wheels clean then repeat using a different color. Tape a photo inside when the paint has dried.

MACK'S TOP TIP:
YOU CAN PUT ANY PICTURE IN YOUR FRAME. YOUR BEST FRIEND, YOUR FAVORITE BAND, OR EVEN YOUR FAVORITE TRUCK!

LIGHTNING BOLT KEY CHAIN

This cool looking key chain is very flashy! Make it, paint it, wear it!

1

Mix up 2 cups of plain flour and 1 cup of salt in a mixing bowl. Add 1 cup of water, and 1 tablespoon oil to make a dough.

YOU WILL NEED

SALT DOUGH RECIPE:	OTHER:
2 CUPS PLAIN FLOUR	PAPER
1 CUP OF SALT	PENCIL
1 CUP OF WATER	A ROLLING PIN
1 TABLESPOON OF COOKING OIL	A KNIFE
	PENCIL
	A BAKING TR
	PAINT
	A KEY CHAIN

2

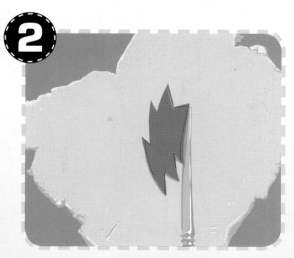

Knead the dough into a ball on a floured work surface. Roll it out to 1½ inch thick. Place a card lightning shape onto the rolled dough and cut around it.

3

Make a small hole in the middle using the tip of a pencil. Set hard. It may take a couple of days to dry out thoroughly or you can oven dry in three hours at a very low temperature.

Paint the lightning bolt in yellow and red. Allow to dry before attaching to a key chain.

LIGHTNING'S TOP TIP: HANG THIS KEY CHAIN FROM YOUR FAVORITE BACKPACK, OR EVEN FROM YOUR PENCIL CASE!

BIGGEST FAN POSTER

Are you Lightning's number one fan like Mia and Tia? To show your appreciation make this fan poster and put it up on your bedroom wall.

YOU WILL NEED

A BIG PIECE OF CARD FOR THE BANNER 20 X 28 INCHES

CARDSTOCK - FOR THE HANDLES

FOIL

THIN CARD FOR THE LETTERS

SAFETY SCISSORS

PENCIL

RULER

GLUE AND CLEAR TAPE

1

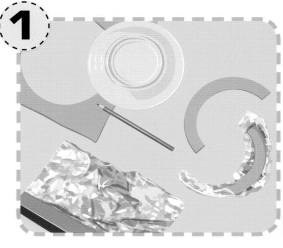

Draw a circle around a plate onto thick card then cut it out. Cut the circle into two handle shapes for the banner. Brush with glue, then cover with foil.

2

LIGHTNING McQUEEN IS MY CHAMP!

(25)

Draw a grid on paper made up of same sized rectangles. Draw out the first letter inside the rectangle. Cut it out.

3

Do the same for the other letters. If you draw them all inside the rectangles they will be the same size.

4

Glue the letters onto the cardboard to spell out your message. Put it up on your wall for everyone to see!

MIA AND TIA'S TOP TIP: MAKE SURE YOU USE BRIGHT PAPER FOR YOUR POSTER. YOU WANT IT TO STAND OUT ON YOUR WALL!

RACE AND PLAY MAT

Mater loves his home town of Radiator Springs. When you've made this play mat you'll love it just as much as him!

YOU WILL NEED

- A FABRIC TWIN SHEET
- ACRYLIC PAINTS
- CARDBOARD
- MASKING TAPE
- PENCIL
- PAINTS
- BRUSHES AND SPONGES
- SAFETY SCISSORS
- FABRIC PENS/FELT PENS

1

Spread the sheet out over some newspaper with a big piece of cardboard underneath (cut from a box). Draw the outline of the roads in pencil then fill in with paint. Dry.

Kids

2

Paint yellow lines onto the roads. Allow to dry thoroughly. It will dry more quickly if you hang it outside on a clear day, on a clothes line.

3

Cut simple card shapes for buildings, trees, and rocky shapes. Stick card strips to the back so they stand up.

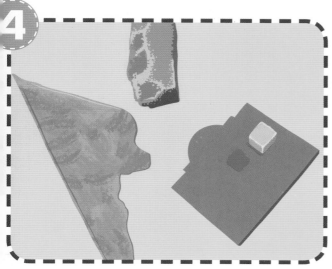

Use small pieces of sponge for printing the windows onto the buildings. Sponge texture onto the rocks and trees. Set your play mat out and get ready for a *Cars* adventure!

MATER'S TOP TIP:
YOUR PLAY MAT IS YOUR OWN NEW RACING WORLD, SO YOU CAN MAKE IT HOW YOU WANT IT! YOU'RE KING OF THE ROAD!

PODIUM BOOKENDS

Chick Hicks knows how to show off on the racetrack, now you can show off your books and cool stuff with these bookends!

YOU WILL NEED

- 3 SMALL BOXES
- TAPE (PREFERABLY MASKING TAPE)
- GLUE AND SAFETY SCISSORS
- LARGE STONES
- PAINT
- COLORED CARD

1

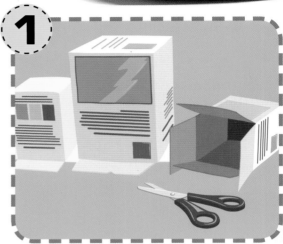

Place the three boxes for your podium together to check the sizes for positions 1, 2 and 3 on the podium. Cut them down if you need to, leaving flaps.

Kids 2

Put a pebble inside each box then tape the flaps securely so the pebbles won't fall out. If the flaps aren't big enough, tape a piece of card to cover the end.

Kids 3

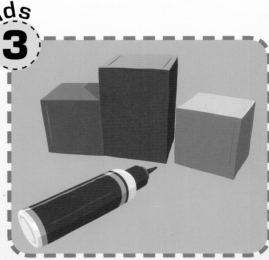

Paint the boxes and allow them to dry. Glue the three boxes together. Position the largest box in the middle and the two smaller ones on either side.

YOU CAN DISPLAY YOUR FAVOURITE TOYS ON THE PODIUMS!

4

Cut out numbers 1, 2, and 3 from the yellow card, then stick them onto the boxes. Or you could cut a circle from card and draw the numbers in felt pen.

BOOK OF COOL STUFF

The King collects cool mementos from his racing wins in a scrapbook. Make your own book of cool stuff whether it's racing themed or just stuff you really like!

YOU WILL NEED

- A SCRAPBOOK
- CARDBOARD BOX OR CEREAL BOX IS FINE
- MASKING TAPE
- TORN PAPER STRIPS
- CORRUGATED CARDBOARD
- OLD NEWSPAPERS OR MAGAZINES
- PAINTS
- STENCIL LETTERS
- SPONGE
- GLUE
- SAFETY SCISSORS

Kids 1

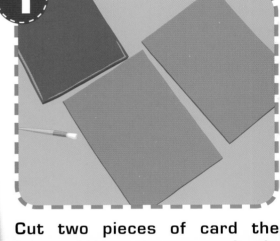

Cut two pieces of card the same size as your scrapbook. Paint them blue and allow to dry.

2

Glue one piece of card to the front of the scrapbook and one piece to the back. Tape down the spine.

Kids 3

Sponge paint onto the corrugated cardboard. Use this to print a pattern onto the paper strips. Sponge paint through the stencil lettering onto strips. Allow to dry.

4

Glue the printed strips of paper onto the front of your scrapbook. Add some torn pieces of newspaper or old magazines to finish off your cool design.

CAR-RAZY CHECKERED POSTER

Want to make your room a racing haven? Then make this checkered wall art and place on your walls!

1

Cut a potato in half. Cut the end of one half into a square. Make the square about 1 x 1 inches.

YOU WILL NEED

LONG 30 INCHES STRIPS OF PAPER - RED AND WHITE

A POTATO

A KNIFE

PAINT

RULER

PENCIL

2

Measure out a long strip of white paper, make it four times wider than the potato square. Measure out two strips of red paper, make them the same width as the potato square.

Kids

3

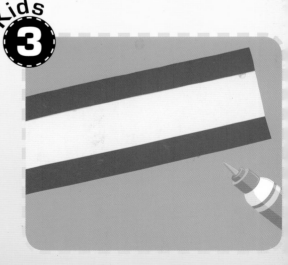

Stick the red strips onto either side of the white strip.

18

LIGHTNING'S TOP TIP:
RACING ISN'T JUST BLACK
AND WHITE. YOU COULD
TRY DIFFERENT CONTRASTING
COLOURS FOR YOUR FLAG.

Dip the square potato block into black paint and print squares onto the strips. Dry. Then position and place the flag on your wall!

STRIKING T-SHIRT

This t-shirt makes an impact and what's the best thing about it? The fact that you designed it and made it yourself! It's an original just like Ramone!

YOU WILL NEED

- A PLAIN T-SHIRT
- TAPE
- CARD - TO GO INSIDE T-SHIRT
- PENCIL
- SAFETY SCISSORS
- THIN CARD STOCK TO MAKE STENCIL
- SPONGE PIECES
- FABRIC PAINTS
- FABRIC PEN FOR OUTLINING IN BLACK
- BUBBLE WRAP

1

Push a piece of card inside the T-shirt. Make sure there are no creases.

2

Draw a big lightning bolt shape onto card. Make sure it will fit the shape of your T-shirt then cut it out so you have a stencil.

3 Kids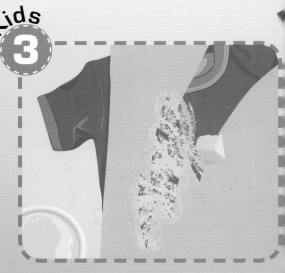

Tape the card stencil over the T-shirt. Dip a sponge into yellow paint, dab it onto newspaper so the paint isn't too wet, then sponge over the lightning strike.

RAMONE'S TOP TIP:
REMEMBER YOU CAN BE INSPIRED BY ANYTHING AROUND YOU! IF YOU LIKE IT, DESIGN IT!

Sponge orange paint onto some bubble wrap and press it down over the top of the lightning shape to make a dotted pattern. Dry and outline the lightning bolt in a black fabric pen.

DVD HOLDER

Create this cool DVD holder inspired by the one and only electric blue D.J.

YOU WILL NEED

A CARDBOARD BOX – CHOOSE A BOX SLIGHTLY BIGGER THAN THE DEPTH OF A DVD.

GLUE

CARD STOCK – A CEREAL BOX IS A GOOD THICKNESS.

PAINT

SAFETY SCISSORS

BRUSH

FOIL

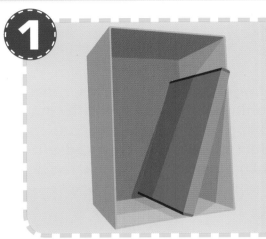

1

Cut a cardboard box to the right size for a DVD to fit inside, leaving a small gap at the top.

Kids

2

Paint the box – bright blue on the outside and then dark blue inside. Dry.

3

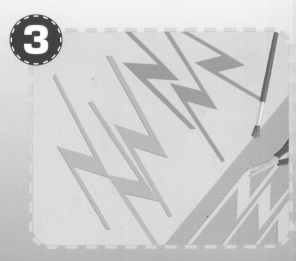

Cut some long Z-shaped pieces from card stock. Paint them in two different greens. Dry.

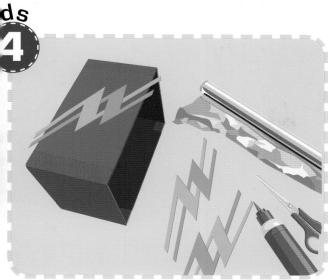

Glue foil strips around the edges of the box. Glue the green Z's to the box. Now you're all set to put your most favorite DVD's inside!

D.J.'S TOP TIP:
YOU COULD MAKE ANOTHER BOX TO STORE YOUR BEST GAMES TOO! ONE FOR EACH.

COIN KEEPER

Sally gave up her super rich lifestyle to live in Radiator Springs, but she still needs somewhere to keep her coins safe!

You will need

- EMPTY CARDBOARD CONTAINER WITH LID
- RULER AND PENCIL
- SEVERAL 8½ X 11 INCH SHEETS OF COLORED PAPER
- WHITE GLUE AND BRUSH
- CRAFT KNIFE OR BOX CUTTER

1

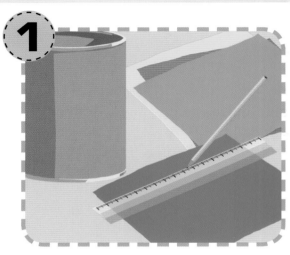

Measure the height of the container and cut the paper to the same height. Draw narrow and wide lines down one sheet.

2

Put the ruled sheet with the lines drawn on it on top of the others and cut along the lines to make long, thin strips.

Kids 3

Paint the strips with glue and stick them to the can, making sure they overlap and smoothing them down carefully.

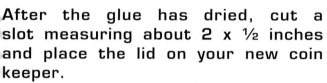

After the glue has dried, cut a slot measuring about 2 x ½ inches and place the lid on your new coin keeper.

SALLY'S TOP TIP:
IF YOU DON'T LIKE THE IDEA OF MULTI-COLORS ON YOUR COIN KEEPER TRY JUST A COUPLE OR EVEN ONE!

SECRET BOOK BOX

Sheriff has to keep a lot of case facts secret and safe. Keep your secrets inside this cool box!

YOU WILL NEED

EMPTY CEREAL BOX

8½ X 11 INCHES OF WHITE CARDBOARD

SAFETY SCISSORS

PENCIL AND RULER

WHITE GLUE AND BRUSH

RED RIBBON

BLACK PAINT

RED AND BLACK CARD

1

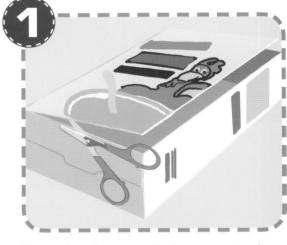

Cut the front of the empty box around three sides. Leave the left side uncut so it makes a flap.

Kids

2

Using the pencil and ruler, draw lines on the white cardboard. Using the box as a guide, cut out three pieces of cardboard to fit around the sides of the box. Glue them in place.

3

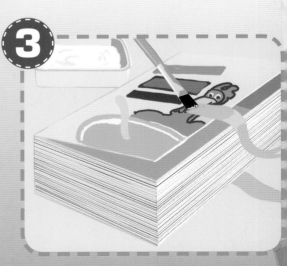

Cut the ribbon in half and glue one piece to the back of the box and the other to the front flap, halfway down.

4

5

Paint the box on the front and spine in black paint. Allow to dry. Paint the back of the box black. Allow to dry.

Cut out a rectangle of red card stock to cover the spine. Cut out a black rectangle and glue to the spine. Cut out a red rectangle and slightly smaller black rectangle from the card for the front of the box. Glue the red card to the front. Dry. Then glue the black on top of the red card. Dry.

SHERIFF'S TOP TIP:
WANT TO ADD A BOLT OF COLOR? ADD COOL DETAILS TO YOUR BOX LIKE THIS FLASH OF LIGHTNING!

FLAMING HOT SHOES

These TOTALLY cool shoes have the hottest design on them, literally!

1

Use the paint to draw and color pictures on your sneakers. Here are scary skulls. Boo! Let dry.

YOU WILL NEED

PAIR OF CLEAN SNEAKERS OR CANVAS SHOES

FABRIC PAINTS

FABRIC PENS

Kids
2

Next, add some more detail in a different colored paint, like these flames. Let dry.

Kids
3

Once you've finished your design on both shoes, allow them to dry thoroughly.

4

Sometimes the paint shrinks a little as it dries and flakes off. Touch up with some fresh paint or fabric paints!

5

Leave your shoes to dry in a cool dry place. Now you're ready to wear your totally unique footwear.

RAMONE'S TOP TIP:
MAKE SURE YOU REALLY PLAN YOUR DESIGN FIRST SO YOU ARE TOTALLY HAPPY WITH THE FINISH!

DOOR HANGER

Wingo's body art is loud and proud and so is this door hanger! Hang this from your bedroom door with pride!

YOU WILL NEED

- BLACK AND RED CARD
- GLUE AND SAFETY SCISSORS
- STRAWS
- SPONGE
- PAINT
- YELLOW PAPER
- PRE-CUT FOAM LETTERS

Kids 1

Glue some plastic straws onto a strip of card. Sponge black paint onto the straws and print a striped pattern onto yellow paper. Dry.

2

Arrange the foam letters to spell out your message. Cut a piece of (red) card big enough for the message to fit on, then glue down the letters leaving a space at the top.

Kids 3

Cut out a circle of black card. Use the straws to print a tire pattern around the edge of the circle. Dip them in paint and print. Allow to dry.

Glue strips cut from the yellow stripy paper around the edge. Glue the tire at the top. Cut a hole into the middle so it can be hung onto a door handle.

WINGO'S TOP TIP:
MAKE SURE A GROWN UP HELPS YOU WITH THE LETTERS. OR YOU COULD JUST WRITE DIRECTLY ONTO YOUR HANGER.

PIT STOP CREW

DO NOT ENTER

PENCIL POT

Keep all your brightest colored pencils or crayons in this pot. Can your pencils compete with Snot Rod's fiery body art?

YOU WILL NEED

EMPTY CARDBOARD TUBE

ABOUT 30 ICE-CREAM STICKS OF THE SAME SIZE

SMALL SET SQUARE (TRIANGLE)

WHITE GLUE AND BRUSH

SNOT ROD'S TOP TIP: ADD SOME COLOR DECORATE WITH PAINTS OR STICKERS!

1

Line up the set square against the tube and glue a stick in place, aligning it with the set square. Let dry.

Kids

2

Glue the sticks around the tube, until it's completely covered. Make sure the sticks align snugly.